MW01537692

This Book belongs to :

_____

Enjoying this notebook?

Please give a review because we would love to hear your feedback, opinions and advice to create better products and services.
Thank you so much for your support.

You are greatly appreciated!

TO DO LIST

TO DO LIST

-
-
-
-
-
-
-
-
-
-
-
-
-
-
-
-
-
-
-
-
-
-
-
-
-
-
-
-
-
-

PASSWORD LIST

PASSWORD LIST

SHOPPING LIST

-
-
-
-
-
-
-
-
-
-
-
-
-
-
-
-
-
-
-
-
-
-
-
-
-
-
-
-

SHOPPING LIST

-
-
-
-
-
-
-
-
-
-
-
-
-
-
-
-
-
-
-
-
-
-
-
-
-
-
-
-
-
-
-

Notes

date_____

Notes

date_____

Notes

date_____

Notes

date_____

Notes

date_____

Notes

date_____

_____

_____

_____

_____

_____

_____

_____

_____

_____

_____

_____

_____

_____

_____

_____

_____

_____

_____

_____

Notes

date_____

Notes

date_____

Notes

date_____

Notes

date_____

Notes

date_____

Notes

date_____

Notes

date_____

Notes

date_____

_____

_____

_____

_____

_____

_____

_____

_____

_____

_____

_____

_____

_____

_____

_____

_____

_____

_____

Notes

date_____

Notes

date_____

Notes

date_____

Notes

date_____

_____

_____

_____

_____

_____

_____

_____

_____

_____

_____

_____

_____

_____

_____

_____

_____

_____

_____

Notes

date_____

_____

Notes

date_____

Notes

date_____

Notes

date_____

Notes

date_____

Notes

date_____

Notes

date_____

Notes

date_____

Notes

date_____

Notes

date_____

Notes

date_____

Notes

date_____

Notes

date_____

Notes

date_____

Notes

date_____

Notes

date_____

Notes

date_____

Notes

date_____

Notes

date_____

Notes

date_____

Notes

date_____

Notes

date_____

Notes

date_____

Notes

date_____

Notes

date_____

Notes

date_____

Notes

date_____

Notes

*date*_____

Notes

date_____

Notes

date_____

Notes

date_____

Notes

date_____

Notes

date_____

Notes

date_____

Notes

date_____

Notes

date_____

Notes

date_____

Notes

date_____

Notes

date_____

Notes

date_____

Notes

date_____

Notes

date_____

Notes

date_____

Notes

date_____

Notes

date_____

Notes

date_____

Notes

date_____

Notes

date_____

Notes

date_____

Notes

date_____

Notes

date_____

Notes

date_____

Notes

date_____

Notes

date_____

Notes

date_____

Notes

*date*_____

Notes

date_____

Notes

date_____

_____

_____

_____

_____

_____

_____

_____

_____

_____

_____

_____

_____

_____

_____

_____

_____

_____

_____

_____

_____

Notes

date_____

Notes

date_____

Notes

*date*_____

Notes

date_____

_____

_____

_____

_____

_____

_____

_____

_____

_____

_____

_____

_____

_____

_____

_____

_____

_____

Notes

date_____

Notes

date_____

Notes

date_____

Notes

date_____

Notes

date_____

Notes

date _____

Notes

date_____

Notes

date_____

Notes

date_____

Notes

date_____

Notes

date_____

Notes

date_____

Notes

date_____

Notes

date_____

Notes

date_____

Notes

date_____

Notes

date_____

Notes

date_____

Notes

date_____

_____
_____
_____
_____
_____
_____
_____
_____
_____
_____
_____
_____
_____
_____
_____
_____
_____
_____
_____
_____

Notes

date_____

_____
_____
_____
_____
_____
_____
_____
_____
_____
_____
_____
_____
_____
_____
_____
_____
_____
_____
_____
_____
_____
_____
_____

Made in the USA
Las Vegas, NV
25 February 2022

44569052R00065